S0-CCE-140

STRESS MANAGEMENT
FOR WOMEN

by *Nancy J. Sullivan, M.A., B.S.N.*

SkillPath Publications, Inc.
Mission, KS

Editor: Kelly Scanlon

Cover Design, Page Design, and Text Layout: Rod Hankins

ISBN: 1-878542-36-2

Printed in the United States of America

STRESS MANAGEMENT
FOR WOMEN

―――――――――

"Woman must come of age by herself…to stand alone…not to depend on another, nor to feel she must prove her strength by competing with another. …She must find her true center alone. She must become whole."

Anne Morrow Lindbergh
from *Gift From the Sea*

TABLE OF CONTENTS

TABLE OF EXERCISES

PREFACE

This is a book for women about managing stress. Never before have women seen such a variety of opportunities for fulfillment and success. Yet these very opportunities bring challenges that pull us and distract us from ourselves, creating stress in our lives.

Awareness is the first step in managing your stress. You may be surprised to discover how big a role stress plays in your life. You can become so accustomed to certain stressors that after awhile, you don't even notice them—they become part of your routine. But that doesn't mean that stress isn't taking its toll on you.

Realize as you read this book and adopt its techniques that the goal is to manage your stress, not to eliminate it. The book is designed to help you understand your body's response to stress and to identify your internal and external stressors. There is also a chapter that focuses on stressors that are unique to women. Finally, this book provides several techniques and strategies for managing stress so that you can move through all the challenges and changes in your life calmly and confidently.

There are many excellent books written on diet and exercise, time management, assertiveness training, and difficult relationships, all of which are helpful in dealing with external stressors. But most of the techniques for managing stress described in this book are about going inside and creating calm and peace from within. This requires you to rely on yourself—to develop your own inner strengths and, most importantly, to get to know yourself. Through these techniques, you will learn to find the place of inner calm that each of us has but often can't find because of the world's distractions. The goal of this book is to help you find that place of inner calm so that you can live a peaceful, productive life.

Nancy Sullivan

UNDERSTANDING YOUR BODY'S REACTION TO STRESS

Expanded roles,
opportunities,
challenges, and changes
offer women exciting
new ways to live, to
develop themselves,
and to find meaning in
their lives. But these
very positive things can
also create great
amounts of stress...

Chapter 1

This is the most exciting time in history to be alive and to be a woman. Never before have so many opportunities been available to women. There are women leaders in every field imaginable—from science to politics, from religion to medicine, from education to business, and throughout the arts.

All the while, the world has never moved faster. The speed at which change can now occur because of technological advances is astronomical. Yet some things, like a woman's love and desire to care for her family to the best of her ability, remain as they always have been—close to her heart.

These expanded roles, opportunities, challenges, and changes offer women exciting new ways to live, to develop themselves, and to find meaning in their lives. But these very positive things can also create great amounts of stress for women. Far beyond seeking food, shelter, and protection for herself and her children, the modern woman is beset with schedules, deadlines, job and career pressures, relationship issues, and health concerns never recognized or acknowledged before.

In 1956, in his book *The Stress of Life,* Hans Selye defined stress as a "nonspecific response to stimuli, internal and external." What are some of those nonspecific ways the body responds to stress? Here are a few (you could even consider them warning signs of stress):

- Headaches
- Insomnia
- Nightmares
- Compulsive overeating
- Loss of interest in sex
- Trouble concentrating
- High blood pressure
- Hives
- Diarrhea

If you are experiencing any of these signs or symptoms, you should know that, first of all, you are not alone. The vast majority of visits to the doctor's office are stress-related. Even the women around you who look so "together" every single time you see them may be secretly suffering from migraine headaches and insomnia.

Second, there are several proven techniques you can use to control your body's response to both internal and external stimuli that cause stress. Most of the tactics for managing stress described in this book are about going inside yourself and creating calm and peace from within. This requires you to rely on yourself. Essentially, these techniques empower you to take control of yourself and your situation.

The Stress Response

The way your body responds to a stressful stimuli or event is actually an example of the wonderful miracle that the body is. Consider the stressful experience that follows. Notice what happens inside your body in response to the events.

At 4:00 o'clock in the morning, you are awakened by your neighbor's dog, Fido, who is barking unbelievably loud. This dog is a huge and mean Doberman pinscher. You are tired, in desperate need of sleep, and the dog will not shut up. You cannot believe your neighbor doesn't hear the beast. You call his house and get the answering machine—no help at all. After 45 minutes, you go outside to knock on your neighbor's door.

Now, this animal is truly dangerous. He not only is kept behind a fence but also has a choke collar and chain that keep him safely tethered to a tree because he can easily jump the fence. Another salient point is that you hate the dog and he hates you. The one thing that really irritates Fido is for someone to run a stick along the fence. That particular noise makes him crazy.

So here you are—it's 4:45 in the morning, you're tired, you're mad, you're walking past Fido and, lo and behold, there's a stick on the ground. You pick up the stick and begin to run it along the fence as you walk to your neighbor's door. Fido growls fiercely and lunges angrily towards you. To your horror, you notice that at this early morning hour, he is not wearing a choke collar.

Okay, now get ready to experience the stress response! In the instant of a true physical threat, your body begins a myriad of physical responses:

- Your heart rate increases.
- Your respiratory rate increases.
- Digestion stops.
- Your hands and feet get cooler.
- The hair on your arms may stand up.
- The pupils of your eyes dilate.
- Your blood pressure increases.

Your body has just brilliantly prepared you to fight Fido or to run from him. It has released a flood of hormones, primarily cortisol, which is closely related to cortisone. Blood has been shunted away from your hands, feet, and digestive tract and pushed to your heart, lungs, and major muscles. Your blood pressure is up. You are stronger and faster now—and ready to take on Fido.

This entire response, *The Alarm Reaction*, is the first phase in what Selye named the *General Adaptation Syndrome* (GAS; see Table 1). [1]

1   Hans Selye, M.D., *The Stress of Life* (New York: McGraw-Hill, 1956), 163.

TABLE 1. Characteristics of the Stages of the
General Adaptation Syndrome

Stage	Characteristics
The Alarm Reaction	Heart rate increases
	Respiratory rate increases
	Digestion ceases
	Hands and feet become cool
	Hair on arms may stand up
	Pupils of eyes dilate
	Blood pressure increases
Stage of Resistance	Chronic release of cortisol
Stage of Exhaustion	Corticoid production decreases
	Death

The second phase, the *Stage of Resistance,* is characterized by the chronic release of hormonal steroid substances in response to the stress. The primary steroid released is cortisol, which suppresses the immune system. Prolonged levels of elevated cortisol are the byproduct of physical and emotional distress.

Elevated cortisol levels are present in the diseases of adaptation, which make up the bulk of modern medical practice. These diseases, generally known as chronic disease, embrace the whole spectrum of medicine and involve every medical specialty, from internal medicine, dermatology, virology, psychiatry, neurology, and gynecology to oncology and premature aging. The implication is that prolonged stress, with no relief, depletes the body's natural healing forces and disease results. Elevated cortisol levels are present in people who have health problems such as high blood pressure, migraine headaches, depression, cancer, heart disease, alcoholism, senility, and chronic pain, just to name a few.

The third and final phase of Seyle's General Adaptation Syndrome is the *Stage of Exhaustion*. Here, corticoid production is depressed to a nil and death occurs. Essentially, the body wears out from being "at peak" for so long.

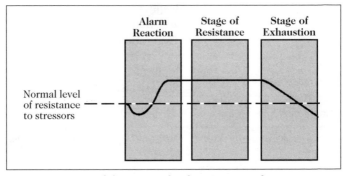

Figure 1. Stages of the General Adaptation Syndrome

So, what starts out as the body's brilliant response to protect and defend itself when threatened can result in death.

So far, you have seen how physical threats to the body can trigger the General Adaptation Syndrome. Take that one step further. Can nonphysical threats also trigger the GAS? Yes. For example, imagine that on its way to you right now is a letter from your friends at the Internal Revenue Service. They think you owe them some money, lots of money, in back taxes. They want to audit you, which means looking at every piece of paper you have touched in the past five years. And don't forget, you may have accrued penalties and interest.

Does this audit pose a physical threat to you? No. But, does your body respond physiologically with a stress response? Yes. Why? Because even if you don't owe the IRS a dime, being audited is going to cost you time and energy, which you probably can't afford to give up.

Here are some other examples of stressors, or challenging life experiences, that you may respond to physically:

- Your teenager staying out all night
- Your husband complaining of chest pain
- Your six-year-old not wanting to go to school because no one likes her
- Your company dropping hints about transferring you to another city

Yes, indeed, you lead an exciting life—whether you realize it or not. But, before you get discouraged, you should know that it is possible to accomplish the things you want to without getting too overwhelmed—and to stay well while you accomplish them. But first, you must review how your nervous system works.

The Nervous System

As you may well know, your body has a system of fibers that electrochemical currents pass through. This system, called the *nervous system,* allows you to do everything from wiggle your toes to swallow. The two major groups of the nervous system are the *voluntary* nervous system and the *involuntary* nervous system.

The voluntary nervous system consists of all the nerves you can voluntarily control. Standing up, sitting down, yelling, blinking, walking, and scratching are just a few of the incredible things you can do at will.

As mentioned, you also have an involuntary nervous system. Right now, could you quit digesting the last meal you ate? Or could you slow your heart rate on command? Can you warm your toes at will? The million dollar name for the involuntary nervous system is the *autonomic* nervous system. This system has two branches, the *sympathetic* and the *parasympathetic*. These two branches have opposite functions; they can never both be "on" at the same time. When one of these two branches of the nervous system is increasing activity, the other one is not.

The sympathetic nervous system gets turned on whenever you are threatened. It is your body's system for preparing you to deal with a threat or stress. The parasympathetic nervous system runs alongside the sympathetic nervous system but is involved in replenishment of self, relaxation, and rebuilding.

The nervous system is another example of the truly amazing design of your body—and it plays a key role in stress management. Table 2 highlights the activities of the nervous system.

TABLE 2. Activities of the Nervous System

VOLUNTARY		
Stand Up	Cross your legs	
Yell	Nod	
Swallow	Scratch	

INVOLUNTARY (AUTONOMIC)		
	Sympathetic	Parasympathetic
Heart rate	↑	↓
Airway size	↑	↓
Blood pressure	↑	↓
Pupil size	↑	↓
Stomach motility	↓	↑
Stomach secretions	↓	↑
Blood vessel size	↓	
Erection of hair	↑	
Local sweating	↑	

If you study Table 2, you'll notice that when the sympathetic nervous system is active, your body responds as it did during that close encounter with Fido. Remember, this system is turned on whenever there is a threat to self. This is Phase 1 of Hans Seyle's General Adaptation Syndrome: Alarm!!! It is a wonderful adaptive response unless it is prolonged or continual. When it is prolonged, it can lead to death.

How can you turn this system off and get control of your stress? By increasing the activity of the parasympathetic nervous system. When the parasympathetic nervous system is "on," the activity of the sympathetic nervous system decreases.

Let's look carefully at the parasympathetic system. When it is active, blood pressure decreases, heart rate decreases, and stomach motility and stomach secretions increase, which means you can digest food. This system is turned "on" when you eat, when you sleep, and when you are relaxed. It is at this time that your body replenishes itself, that immune cells divide and multiply. This system is also activated when there is sexual activity.

Some of the tools used to manage stress are essentially techniques for activating the parasympathetic nervous system, which elicits a relaxation response. To better understand how to activate this system, let's look at the connection between the mind and the body.

The Mind/Body Connection

More than three centuries ago, on the morning of November 10, 1619, a French philosopher, René Descartes, awoke from a dream that inspired his lifelong philosophical work. The essence of this work was that the mind and the body are separate. This was to become a principle on which the current medical model of health care is based. In this way of thinking, the body is a biochemical machine separate from the thoughts and feelings the individual experiences.

Even so, everyone has experienced the intricate connection between the mind and the body. Consider blushing, for example. Think about it—a mental stimuli, an image, or a comment can actually make your skin change color. Although you may be aware of this connection between your mind and your body and experience it thousands of times, like many people, you may dismiss it when it comes to considering its impact on your health.

Some of the strongest evidence of the mind/body connection can be seen in the field of surgery. When patients come to the hospital for an operation, they sign a permit, hand over their car keys, put on a hospital gown, and allow themselves to be put under anesthesia. Then an incision is made and something is taken out or put in. Next, the incision is closed and the patient is awakened and told, "Okay, now you're fixed."

The questions for those in the mind/body field always are:

1. How does that incision know how to heal?
2. Why sometimes when patients should recover, they don't?

Consider, for example, that if people were machines like cars, then emotions like fear, depression, loneliness, hope, and love wouldn't affect the healing process. But they do. Some people for whom everything goes technically perfect die anyway. Other people experience everything that could possibly go wrong—bleeding, infection, medical equipment malfunction, and other complications—yet recover wonderfully. What makes the difference? According to many experts, the influence of the mind.

Candice Pert, Ph.D., of the National Institute of Mental Health in Bethesda, Maryland, is joined by other researchers around the country who are discovering that the mind is located throughout the body. Pert and her colleagues are pioneers in a whole new field called *psychoneuroimmunology,* which is the study of how psychology—how a person thinks and feels—affects brain chemistry and how that then affects the immune system. Many patients are learning to impact their health with interventions like stress management and visualization.

One example of this powerful link between your thoughts and your body is the *placebo effect.* You probably know what a placebo is. It is an inert substance or sham procedure that produces the desired effect when applied or ingested. For a drug to get through the FDA, it must be better than placebo. Generally speaking, 28 percent to 33 percent of people treated with placebo will have positive results; that is, a thought or an image will physically alter the body one-third of the time.

Another dramatic example of the mind/body connection is seen in people with Multiple Personality Disorder, or MPD. MPD is much more commonly reported now, as are the circumstances thought to give rise to it—child abuse. Some victims of abuse learn to dissociate and turn off their core personality when the suffering is too great. They create another personality to take the abuse. When the abuse is too great for the second personality, they create a third, and so forth, which allows the original child to eat, sleep, kiss Mommy and Daddy good night, live and grow up. This is a pretty ingenious psychological adaptative process— don't you think?

Studies have found that people with MPD may be allergic in one personality, but not in another; may exhibit burns in one personality, but not in another; may display drug reactions in one personality, but not in another; or may switch from being right-handed to being left-handed in different personalities. This tells us that certain physical traits that we thought were fixed—diabetes, left- or righthandedness, allergies, and color blindness, to name a few—may not be, lending support to the mind/body connection.

Body and mind are different expressions of the same information. This information is carried by chemical transmitters called *peptides*, which are the messenger molecules. They carry information between the brain and the organs and cells of the body in a never-ending feedback loop. This is why we blush when we are embarrassed.

It used to be thought that communication between the brain and the body was mainly one way, brain to body. Recent findings make it clear that the communication is reciprocal. But many people have grown deaf to these inner promptings. Stress management is about learning to get quiet enough to hear your body. One way to do this is to quiet the mind so that you can hear the body. Another way is to relax the body and allow the mind to become calm. You'll learn about these stress management tools in Chapter 3.

That which calms the body calms the mind, and whatever calms the mind also calms the body.

THE SPECIAL STRESSORS OF WOMEN

"Women...must contend with special inner stressors that they may not even be aware of. These stressors relate to body image, self-esteem, and self-perception..."

Chapter 2

Now that you know the way your body reacts to stress, let's take a look at some of the forms of stress you encounter on a daily basis. Although your daily schedule and immediate worries account for a large part of your stress, other causes of stress may be more subtle. Women, especially, must contend with special inner stressors that they may not even be aware of. These stressors relate to body image, self-esteem, and self-perception—do you feel in control of yourself and your schedule, or do you feel like a victim?

To begin identifying your stressors, complete Exercise 1. It contains the *QuikGuide to Measuring and Managing Your Stress*,[2] which is based on a scientifically devised stress scale called *The Inventory of Stressors*. Please note that no test is perfectly accurate and that a thorough assessment is best done with the help of a professional. This test is for your own use and will give you a good idea of your stress patterns.

---

2   Charles L. Sheridan, *The QuikGuide to Measuring and Managing Your Stress*. (Overland Park, KS: The Creative Mind, 1987). Used with permission.

Exercise 1

The QuikGuide to Measuring and Managing Your Stress

Instructions: Place a check mark next to each item that applies to you now or has applied over the last six months or so. If you are not sure how to respond, give the answer that seems to fit you best.

1. ❑ Dealing with my children's problems and questions.
2. ❑ Rarely or never having too much to do.
3. ❑ Feeling accepted by others.
4. ❑ Experiencing high-level noise at work or home.
5. ❑ Having my mother or father say something like "You don't really love me."
6. ❑ Being clear about what is expected of me.
7. ❑ Planning an important contract or piece of work.
8. ❑ Demanding my rights at work.
9. ❑ Feeling I have no real purpose in life.
10. ❑ Having someone call something I've said or done "stupid."
11. ❑ Having my leisure plans upset.
12. ❑ Feeling committed at home or at work.
13. ❑ Not having to cope with bureaucratic machinery.
14. ❑ Having my primary-relationship partner (spouse or mate) stare at a possible rival who seems quite attractive.
15. ❑ Not going along with the group.
16. ❑ Seeing little challenge in my work or play.
17. ❑ Asserting my rights or privileges.
18. ❑ Watching or reading the news.

Exercise 1

Continued

19. ❑ Having someone act as if they dislike me.
20. ❑ Having my sexual needs met.
21. ❑ Being around angry people.
22. ❑ Being watched while I'm working.
23. ❑ Suffering a loss of status.
24. ❑ Having things to do that interest me.
25. ❑ Working or living in situations where things are well-organized.
26. ❑ Watching an argument between members of my family.
27. ❑ Having regular opportunities to express my viewpoint.
28. ❑ Getting to have a good laugh.
29. ❑ Giving a speech before a group of relative strangers.
30. ❑ Having little control over what happens to me.
31. ❑ Making decisions that affect my family's future.
32. ❑ Carrying out work that is mentally demanding.
33. ❑ Rarely or never suffering discomfort or pain.
34. ❑ Finding myself in a position in my primary relationship where anything I say or do will be wrong.
35. ❑ Making major decisions in my life.
36. ❑ Being around people who are talking in a loud voice.
37. ❑ Rarely or never working against a tight deadline.
38. ❑ Experiencing a great deal of family friction.
39. ❑ Feeling angry.
40. ❑ Rarely or never traveling on congested public transport or in traffic jams.

Exercise 1

Continued

41. ❑ Failing or forgetting to perform some important responsibility.
42. ❑ Living a stimulating, interesting life.
43. ❑ Keeping my emotions to myself.
44. ❑ Having opportunities to have fun.
45. ❑ Making decisions independently.
46. ❑ Being interviewed for a job.
47. ❑ Having my abilities at work valued and put to good use.
48. ❑ Being bombarded by questions and requests.
49. ❑ Having sleep patterns that are good and regular.
50. ❑ Having the authority to meet my responsibilities at work.
51. ❑ Having enough time to myself.
52. ❑ Thinking about major problems confronting me.
53. ❑ Angrily telling someone off.
54. ❑ Knowing the end product of my work.
55. ❑ Having variation or fresh stimulation in my sexual activities.
56. ❑ Losing my health and being forced to change my lifestyle.
57. ❑ Being able to perform satisfactorily on my job.
58. ❑ Having to make decisions where I will lose out no matter what I do.
59. ❑ Spending time in work areas or rooms that are drab, uncomfortable, and depressing.
60. ❑ Being in a situation where I am unsure of the right thing to do.
61. ❑ Having thoughts of losing my primary-relationship partner or someone else dear to me.

Exercise 1

Continued

62. ❏ Having enough money to meet expenses.
63. ❏ Moving away from home to a new town.
64. ❏ Losing my job.
65. ❏ Having a nourishing well-balanced diet.
66. ❏ Getting enough exercise.
67. ❏ Having to do jobs I can't cope with.
68. ❏ Rarely or never having to do jobs I have no interest in.
69. ❏ Getting the rewards I had hoped for.
70. ❏ Having a low opinion of myself.
71. ❏ Rarely or never working long hours.
72. ❏ Having enough leisure time.
73. ❏ Being overburdened with responsibility.
74. ❏ Having the opportunity to see friends socially.
75. ❏ Undergoing disruption of my marriage.
76. ❏ Rarely or never having to work at jobs that are too simple for me.
77. ❏ Working at a task that requires constant attention, but leaves little room for initiative.
78. ❏ Having to work with inadequate lighting.
79. ❏ Feeling that something extremely unpleasant could happen to me or to someone close to me and being helpless to do anything about it.
80. ❏ Feeling I have friends or relatives who will help me when I need help.

How to Find Your Stress Rating

A. Some of the test item numbers are circled. For each item with a circled number you did *not* check, add a point to your score. Write in your total number of points here.

_____

B. Now, count the number of items you checked that are *not* circled. For each of these items, add one to your score. Then write in the total points from the uncircled items here.

_____

C. Add point totals for (A) and (B) above to get your stress rating score.

_____

If your score is close to 35, you have an average level of stress in your life. This does not mean that stress is not an important consideration for you, since the average level of stress in our society is quite high.

If your score includes as many as 45 items, you are notably higher on stressors than the average person. Give serious consideration to what you can do to lower your stress rating.

A score of 55 or more indicates a high level of stress. A score this high means it's time to give special attention to lowering your stress levels and/or learning special ways of coping with that stress. Relaxation training and meditation practice are good general antidotes to stress.

Body Image and Stress

One of the major stressors women experience at a very early age is the acceptance of their body. As females, we are almost never willing to accept our bodies as beautiful, or even as okay. This is not a twentieth-century, Western phenomenon. Women throughout time and from a variety of cultures have strived to reach some kind of ideal physical appearance, even to the extreme of self-mutilation.

Aristocratic families in Japan bound the healthy, normal feet of their daughters by the time the children were seven years old. Normal-sized feet were not beautiful. The first bindings were changed when they became too soaked with blood and pus.

In Burma, beauty is achieved by elongating a woman's neck with rings. These rings separate the vertebrae of the neck, making a fracture quite possible should the rings be removed. A normal, healthy neck length is just not quite attractive enough.

Some African women use discs to form large, platypus lips. In this culture, large lips are truly more beautiful than inherited family features.

In the nineteenth century, a very small waist meant a woman was delicate, feminine, and beautiful. So women donned corsets that could weigh up to forty pounds. The weight of these beautifying devices caused digestive tract problems, shortness of breath, and frequently, prolapse of the uterus.

During World War I, the French decided that large breasts were unattractive. It became fashionable for women to tightly bind their chests to appear small-breasted. This, of course, destroyed normal connective supportive tissue, creating breasts that sagged heavily.

For Victorian women it was beautiful to be very pale. To accomplish this, women would ingest chalk or arsenic. This definitely took the color out of their cheeks, sometimes permanently.

In modern Western culture, fleshiness is viewed with disgust and contempt. Women inflict on themselves barbaric dieting, frenetic exercising, and surgery to be "beautiful." Consider this except from an article that appeared in *The Kansas City Star* in August 1993:

> . . . *a 30-year-old woman was admitted to the hospital for increasing pain and swelling in the right thigh. She had a mild fever. The pain limited movement in her right hip. . .*
>
> *One reason the case was so hard to diagnose was that the patient had neglected to tell the doctor a key piece of information: For six weeks she had been using a special device for 15 minutes a day in the belief that it would help her achieve thin thighs.*
>
> *Once she revealed this habit, the diagnosis was made, "thigh thin thecitis." (Thecitis is an inflammation of the covering surrounding the tendon.)*
>
> *Why is this problem so common? Many studies suggest that women's dissatisfaction with their bodies focuses on their hips and thighs. When women lose weight through diet and exercise, fat is lost from storage deposits all over the body. But even when the scale shows that their weight falls within normal range, many think the mirror tells them they have too much padding around the thighs.*

Women's dissatisfaction with their bodies—which spans both cultures and time—seems to grow out of self-shame. In one research project, psychologists gathered two groups of well-educated, healthy adults between the ages of 30 and 50. One group was female and one was male. The subjects were not actors or models; they were average, everyday people. Individuals in each group were asked to describe their physical appearance.

The majority of the males wrote comments such as "tall," "handsome," "great eyes," "strong jaw line," "muscular," "thick hair and broad shoulders." The females described themselves in the following ways: "fat thighs," "wide hips," "too tall," "too short," "prominent nose," and "flat-chested." The males exhibited pride in their bodies and the females shame. Realistically, how many of these men do you think had a potbelly or parted their hair to hide their baldness? Men do care and worry about their appearance, but their sense of value or worthiness throughout time has not depended on it.

The feeling of not being okay, of being ashamed of their physical appearance is a major "silent" stressor in women's lives. It can permeate thoughts and actions, decreasing self-confidence and self-worth.

In his book *Peace, Love and Healing,* Bernie Siegel, M.D., recounts the challenge of one young woman, Evy McDonald, to become "okay within herself." Evy was diagnosed with amyotrophic lateral sclerosis (Lou Gehrig's disease) in 1980. She was told by her neurologist that she had six to twelve months to live and that she should consider donating her body to science. She wrote the following:

There I sat in front of a mirror in my wheelchair. In the six months since I'd been diagnosed as having ALS, my once firm, strong muscles had wasted away into flaccid, useless ones. I was dying from a particularly rapid form of this incurable disease and had, at best, six months to live. I looked with disgust at my deteriorating body. I hated it. The mirrored reflection of one spindly, ill-shaped leg (the legacy of a childhood bout with polio) paired with a mammoth, once muscular one was hideous to me . . .

As the hours of my day were now relegated to sitting alone in my wheelchair, I began to observe rather than react to my thoughts. I noticed there was one consistent thread throughout the fabric of my life—a relentless obsession with weight. I was sure that if I became "skinny" enough, an admirable body would magically greet me in the mirror. And now I sat in a wheelchair with acutely atrophying muscles. My arms and legs were shrinking.

Was it just a coincidence that I'd always wanted a smaller body and that ALS was granting me that very desire? . . .

As I sat in my wheelchair, six months from death, a single, passionate desire pressed to the front of my mind. In my last months of life I wanted to experience unconditional love. I wanted to know that sweetness.

But how could I even hope to realize that goal if I couldn't accept my own body? . . .

The first step was to notice and write down how many negative thoughts I had about my body in the course of each day, and how many positive ones. When I saw the huge preponderance of negative thoughts on the paper, I was forced to confront the degree of hatred I had for my body.

To counter this habitual and ingrained negativity, every day I singled out one aspect of my physical body that was acceptable to me, no matter how small. Next, I'd use that item to begin the rewriting. Every negative thought would be followed by a positive statement like "and my hair is truly pretty," or "I have lovely hands," or "My bright eyes and warm smile light up my face." Each day a different positive item would be added as each day the rewriting continued.

I felt like a jig-saw puzzle being put back together; and when the last bit was in place, my mind shifted and saw the whole perfect picture. I couldn't pinpoint just when the shift occurred, but one day I noticed that I had no negative thoughts about my body. I could look in the mirror at my naked reflection and be honestly awed by its beauty. I was totally at peace, with a complete unalterable acceptance of the way my body was—a bowl of jello in a wheelchair.

For the first time in my life I knew my body to be aesthetically pleasing. A new movie had been written [Evy had earlier referred to the body as "the screen where the movie is shown."] and I experienced a soft, sensuous human being sitting in that wheelchair.

*Once the old scripts and demeaning images
were finally and totally gone, they were never to
emerge again. I accepted my body. It didn't need
to be any different; it could be whatever it was
and become whatever it was to be . . .*

*This was one step in a journey that over time
brought about unexpected and unsolicited
physical improvements.*[3]

The technique that Evy McDonald used, not only to
accept her physical body but to learn to see it as
beautiful, is one that all women should practice and
teach their daughters. The sense of awe at the beauty
that we are given as our birthright should be developed
from the inside. It should not be a reaction to what the
outside world perceives as beautiful.

3 Bernie Siegel, M.D., *Peace, Love and Healing Bodymind Communication and the
Path to Self-Healing: An Exploration* (New York: Harper & Row, 1989), 31-32.

Self-Esteem and Stress

High self-esteem is a very deep sense of unconditional love and respect for one's self. It is a true form of inner power. Lack of self-esteem creates all kinds of stress and pain in women's lives. We are constantly beset with negative ideas and feelings about ourselves. The feeling of unworthiness can manifest itself as anxiety around people whose approval we want, or tasks we feel we could never do well enough. We may question why people in our lives—our husbands or our children—love us. Surely someone else could be a better wife or mother, we may think.

These may be fleeting ideas that occur occasionally, or these thoughts may make up the bulk of our waking hours and haunt us at night. We may compensate by trying to be perfect. Or we may feel like we can never do enough and then exhaust ourselves trying, which leads to anger and frustration. We may avoid the pain of low self-esteem by exhibiting obsessive behaviors. Although this behavior saps our physical and mental energy, it is an excellent distractor from painful and stress-inducing thoughts.

Self-confidence and self-esteem are not the same. As suggested previously, women's shame originates from a sense of self-shame—a sense that somehow, in our essence, we are not okay enough and that we need to do many things to make up for this lack. You may have a lot of self-confidence and still not feel worthy and valuable. Self-confidence is assurance that you can perform the task before you, that you can do what is asked, or that you can reach your own goals. You may come by self-confidence naturally. People with outgoing, aggressive, or assertive personalities tend to be self-confident.

Consider, for example, a group of five-year-olds at a party. One or two children get back in line for another treat before some of the children have gotten their first one. Despite every effort to teach these children manners and self-restraint, their overwhelming sense of eagerness prevails. It's almost as if these children can't help their behavior. These children, by nature, are going to try more things, to take more chances. Because they attempt more, they will have more opportunities to succeed and to develop self-confidence.

But because self-confidence and self-esteem are not the same thing, even the enthusiastic child who grows up and accomplishes many things may not feel truly worthy or of value in the very core of her being without those accomplishments.

Another manner in which people struggle to acquire self-confidence is through association with something that is socially valued. This is an outer form of power, and it is the one most frequently recognized in our culture. You can acquire this sense of power through marriage. Or you can be born into it, or elected to it. You might get it through a promotion. It may come to you in the form of an inheritance. This kind of external power brings with it self-confidence and the sense that "Now I am somebody and I can do or have what I want." The problem with this kind of power is that it can be lost, divorced from, disinherited and, in the case of political power, defeated. It is all acquired by association to something or someone outside of self.

How do you develop high self-esteem? How can you achieve a sense of worthiness and value in the very core of your being? One way is to be lucky enough to be born into a family that extends unconditional love. In such an environment, people love you just because you are you. All you have to do is keep breathing. The acceptance is not based on appearance, talent, intelligence, or behavior—although all of those aspects may be recognized. The acceptance and positive regard are pure. The child takes this in, and living with a love and respect for self becomes the way of being.

Most parents attempt this in their child rearing. For many women, having a child is the first time someone else's heartbeat matters as much to them as their own. As a consequence, mothers pour love into their children. Self-esteem assessment of school children indicates that 95 percent of children entering kindergarten have high self-esteem and that only 5 percent of high school seniors have high self-esteem. What happens?

We live in a society that does not value human life unconditionally. Instead, our society values people based on their accomplishments, intelligence, physical beauty, talent, youth, athletic ability, wealth, and material possessions. When a young girl enters school, the pecking order begins, if it hasn't already started at home. She may easily fall into this value trap and measure her worthiness by it. So even if she is loved unconditionally, it is possible that exposure to society's values and the educational process may diminish her sense of self-worth.

Here are five steps for developing high self-esteem or for building on what you already have. Remember, you can begin these steps at any time in your life—it's never too late. The goal is to give yourself unconditional love. Just as Evy McDonald learned not only to accept but also to *see* her body as beautiful, you can learn to love yourself at a core level.

Steps to Enhancing Self-Esteem

1. Stop criticizing yourself. Criticism doesn't improve things; it only creates worse feelings. We all self-talk—and most of it is negative. Consider, for example, how often you catch yourself saying or thinking things like "My hair looks terrible," "That was a dumb thing to say," "I'm such a klutz," or "I'm lousy at this."

   When you find yourself involved in self-criticism, tell yourself "cancel-cancel."

2. Stop terrifying yourself with scary images. When your mind creates pictures around your vulnerabilities (your husband with another woman, the new employee getting promoted to your job, your child being kidnapped because you're late from work picking him or her up), replace it immediately with an image that is positive to you.

3. Be kind and gentle to yourself. Do not overwork. Do not take on other peoples' responsibilities. Do nice things for yourself. Give yourself enough time to eat, to sleep, to bathe, and to get ready comfortably. Read the book you have been wanting to read. Buy yourself that song on the radio you like so well. Tell people "no" sometimes. Get a massage. All of these are ways to tell yourself, "I love you and you're valuable."

4. Spend time alone. Have a relationship just with yourself. Be with your thoughts and feelings. Take time to listen to your inner promptings. Value this time.

   Do not distract yourself from yourself.

5. Your eyes are directly connected to your brain. A neurological exam always includes looking into the eyes. Every morning when you wake up, go to the mirror, look directly in your eyes, and tell yourself, "I love you unconditionally." This may feel uncomfortable at first. Negative thoughts may enter. Repeat the phrase. Make this a habit whenever you look in a mirror. If you are having a particularly bad day, take a walk. With each step that you take, tell yourself, "I love you."

Extend yourself in love to you.

Stress and Victim-Type Thinking

Victim-type thinking is prevalent in our society. Some sociologists think that now, more than at any other time, people perceive themselves as victims of all kinds of things—crime, bureaucracy, the judicial system, big business, discrimination—the list goes on.

In his book *AIDS: A Passageway for Transformation,* Dr. Norman Shealy, a noted neurosurgeon, correlates various illnesses with what was occurring with the population socially and psychologically at certain points in history. One example that he cites is the correlation between polio and the Great Depression. At that time, the word "crippling" was used to describe the economy. As the country came out of the economic depression and Jonas Salk discovered the polio vaccine, the word "recovery" was used to describe the economy.

Consider the current disease of the day. It is not cancer or heart disease. It is AIDS. A person with AIDS becomes the physical manifestation of victim. He or she

cannot defend against even the slightest onset
of infection.

Researchers have known for a long time that victim-
type thinking suppresses the immune system. Researchers at Harvard University Medical School have
found that the more the nurses like you, the greater
your chance of dying. Two patients with the same
disease and the same prognosis can approach the
illness from two very different perspectives.

Patient A is lying in her hospital bed saying to herself:
"Why me? Bad things just seem to happen to me.
There's nothing that I can do about this. I hope those
doctors and nurses can fix this."

Patient B has been on the nurse call button twelve
times and it's only 10:00 a.m. She wants to know:
"Where is my doctor? And why did you draw that
blood? And what's this medicine for?"

She doesn't wear pajamas at 10:00 a.m. at home, and
she's not going to wear them here. By the way, she
knows that visiting hours haven't started yet, but this is
the only time today that her kids can come and they
are definitely staying. If that's not okay, well, let's just
shut the door, she says. Who do you think the nurses
want to go home? Of course, it's Patient B.

What we learn when we draw blood out of these two
patients who are supposedly in the same situation is
that Patient B's immune system is functioning significantly higher. She has a greater chance of survival.

Exercise 2

Identifying Victim-Type Thinking

1. Make a list of things that would make your life significantly better if you never, ever had to do them again. What goes on the list? Paying taxes? Arguing with your teenager? Dealing with a particular problem or person at work?

   _____   _____
   _____   _____
   _____   _____
   _____   _____
   _____   _____
   _____   _____

2. Now list how these things make you feel. If you take the time to do this exercise with some real thought and consideration, you can gain a clear picture of your perspective in various areas of your life.

   _____   _____
   _____   _____
   _____   _____
   _____   _____
   _____   _____
   _____   _____

How do the items you listed make you feel? Sad? Frustrated? Angry? Out of control? Depressed? Tired? Hopeless? Helpless? These are all terms that describe how a victim feels.

Victim-type thinking is not a health-inducing response to the stress of life. Here are several steps you can take to eliminate this type of thinking:

1. Identify the experiences, relationships, problems, or situations that are making you feel like a victim (helpless and hopeless).

2. Accept total accountability for whatever the problem or situation is. Did you notice how Patient A gave her disease away? She wanted the doctors and nurses to fix it. Patient B wanted to know everything about her treatment and wanted control of the situation.

   So it is with you and your life, your family, your job. These are *your* experiences. Sure, at times those experiences may be difficult. But don't fall into the habit of victim-type thinking—of feeling that those difficult situations are under someone else's control and that you can't do anything to change them. Inside each one is a great pearl of wisdom for you; but you have to be challenged by it, grapple with it, study it, and crack it open to get the pearl out.

   To give away such a treasure would be foolish.

3. Become action-oriented about the difficulty. Move, ask questions, get opinions, read, organize a problem-solving group, write a letter, set goals—do something! What should you do if you take an action to resolve something and nothing happens? Act again. The very process of putting forth energy in a positive way reduces stress and can actually transform the situation.

There is a wonderful story we tell children that is a metaphor for this process. Remember the tale of the frog who is hopping along the road and accidentally hops into a pail of milk? He does not know what to do. He can hope that some small boy will come along and pull him out. He can hope that something knocks the pail over. He can wish that a strong wind would break a limb off a tree and that the branch would land across the pail so that he could climb out. But all that he really has are his legs, so he kicks. And nothing happens. So he kicks again and nothing happens. But he continues to kick and kick and kick and kick. He kicks all night long. The milk is churned into butter and the frog climbs out.

The action that you take on your own behalf may not resolve a situation immediately, but repeated actions can transform you or your situation in ways so subtle that you do perceive the cumulative effect.

A step out of victimhood is always action-oriented.

STRESS MANAGEMENT TOOLS

"Awareness is the first step in managing your stress…you can become so accustomed to certain stressors that after a while, you don't even notice them — they become part of your routine."

Chapter 3

In this chapter, you'll learn specific exercises, tools, and techniques to help you gain control over the stresses of daily life:

- Deep breathing
- Biofeedback
- Meditation/inner silencing
- Self-hypnosis
- Progressive Relaxation
- Sound and music
- Exercise and massage
- Diet and nutrition
- Autogenic training
- The Six-Second Quieting Reflex

Each of these methods is an effective stress management technique. The important thing to remember as you learn about each technique is that the mind and the body are intricately connected.

Deep Breathing

Changes in your breathing patterns are one of your body's nonspecific responses to an internal or external stimuli. Experience any physical or emotional threat and your breathing patterns will immediately change. However, by learning to consciously change your breathing, you can alter your emotions and physical responses. Many of the Eastern traditions regard breathing as the link between the mind and the body.

Most people hold their breath when they're excited, making them more vulnerable. The following steps will help you learn to relax through breathing. Read through the exercise until you are familiar with the steps and then try the exercise.

Exercise 3

Learning Your
Breathing Patterns

Observe your breathing pattern.

Lie on the floor, eyes closed. Don't move.

1. What moves when you breathe?

- Your chest?
- Rib cage?
- Abdomen?

2. Is your breathing shallow, medium, or deep?

3. How fully do you fill your lungs?

4. How many times do you breathe each minute?

5. Are shorter breaths followed by longer ones?

6. Do you breathe through your nose or mouth?

7. Do you use both nasal passages?

Correct breathing does not come from the chest. Abdominal breathing is the most natural form. Find a small child, under the age of four, and observe the child's breathing patterns. Place your hand on the child's chest as he or she breathes. Now place your hand on the child's abdomen. Is the child breathing from the chest or from the abdomen? We have a lot to learn from people who have not stopped listening to their bodies.

Exercise 4

Learning to
Breathe Correctly

Follow these steps to practice correct breathing:

1. Allow air to enter through your nostrils and travel downward, as if to fill your abdomen.

2. Exhale through the mouth until your lungs are as empty as possible and your abdomen is again flat.

3. At this of point of emptiness, close your mouth.

4. Your next breath should arise spontaneously; do not force it.

5. Continue to focus on your breathing with a slow, total inhale and a slow, total exhale.

This is an excellent exercise to practice before facing a situation that requires you to be at your best. Also practice it each night before you go to sleep and every morning when you awaken.

My mind and body are connected.

Biofeedback

Through *biofeedback,* you can learn to control your involuntary nervous system. The method uses monitoring devices and measuring instruments that give you feedback on what's going on inside your body. You can actually learn to "hear" muscle tension and heart rate or "see" skin temperature and brain waves. There is no magic in the machines. The ability to control heart rate or skin temperature is inside you. The machines enhance the body's responses, which allows you to know when you have altered a response. Eventually, you will learn to reproduce the conditions that caused the physical changes.

The Biofeedback Society of America cites scientific research documenting that biofeedback is helpful for individuals who suffer from chronic pain, teeth grinding, high blood pressure, muscle tension headaches, migraine (vascular) headaches, Reynaud's Syndrome, cardiac dysrhythmias, and epileptic seizures.

Biofeedback training usually requires six to eight weekly sessions with a therapist. During these sessions, participants complete an assessment and receive instruction on various relaxation techniques. The training requires daily practicing, monitoring, and recording of progress and results.

With biofeedback training, you can expect a reduction of pain and other symptoms, a decreased reliance on medication, and an increased ability to deeply relax.

Included with this book is a very simple biofeedback device, the Stress Manager Card. To use the device, place your thumb on the square and note the color the square turns.

TABLE 3. Stress Manager Card Ratings

Color	Temperature	Indicates
Amber	79.6°F.	Chronic tension
Yellow Green	81.6°F. 83.6°F.	Nervous
Turquoise Blue Violet	85.6°F. 87.6°F. 89.6°F.	Alert and active
Deep Blue	Above 95.0°F.	Deeply relaxed

According to Table 3, what is your color/hand temperature? Do you feel stressed right now? Use the chart in Exercise 5 to record your color/hand temperature at different times during the day for the next week. Keeping these records will provide you with a picture of your periods of stress. Searching for the causes of your stress and identifying the times of day when you are stressed is the first step in stress management. Examine your temperature chart. You might be very surprised at what you learn. What were you doing during your periods of high stress?

Exercise 5

Recording Your Daily
Biofeedback Temperature

For the next seven days, use the Stress Manager Card to identify your periods of stress. Refer to Table 3 to record the color of the square on the card and its corresponding temperature. For the periods in which you were experiencing high stress, record the activities or thoughts that were the source of your stress.

	After rising in the morning	10 a.m.	2 p.m.	6 p.m.	At bedtime
Day 1					
Day 2					
Day 3					
Day 4					
Day 5					
Day 6					
Day 7					

Meditation/Inner Silencing

Throughout recorded history, almost every culture— from the ancient Egyptians to contemporary Eskimos— have used internal focusing techniques, or various forms of meditation, to achieve a balance between the mind and the body. Meditation quiets the mind and, consequently, relaxes the body.

To achieve a meditative state, you must dwell on something for an extended period of time without "thinking" about it. Meditation may be either *active* or *passive*. In passive meditation, you focus on a special set of words called *mantra,* a sound, your breath, or an object. In active approaches, you immerse yourself in an engaging activity that forces your full attention on that activity. Examples of active meditation are repetitive movement or complex dance.

Here are some tips for meditating:

1. Select the right technique for you:

Passive	*Active*
Words	Movement
Sound	Play
Breath	
Object	

2. Don't meditate when you're tired.

3. Don't meditate when you're angry.

4. Limit the time of your sessions.

5. Eliminate disturbances.

6. Get comfortable.

7. Practice every day for fifteen minutes, at the same time each day.

8. Experiment with other forms of meditation.

In his book *The Relaxation Response,* Dr. Herbert Benson outlines six steps to deep relaxation:

1. Sit quietly in a comfortable position.

2. Close your eyes.

3. Deeply relax all your muscles. You may want to practice Progressive Relaxation (refer to page 50).

4. Breathe through your nose. Become aware of your breathing. As you breathe out, say the word "one" silently to yourself. For example, breathe in...out, "one"; in...out, "one"; over and over again. Breathe easily and naturally from your abdomen (refer to page 38).

5. Continue this process for ten to twenty minutes; open your eyes to check the time, if necessary, but do not use an alarm. When you finish, sit quietly for several minutes—at first with your eyes closed and later with your eyes open.

6. Do not worry about whether you have been success-ful in achieving a deep level of relaxation. Maintain a passive attitude and let the relaxation occur at its own pace. When distracting thoughts occur, try not to dwell on them. Return to repeating "one."

Practice this technique daily, but not within two hours after a meal because the digestive processes seem to interfere with the relaxation response.

When I calm my mind, I relax my body.

Self-Hypnosis

Hypnosis. This mysterious-sounding state is actually a very familiar experience to all of us. Hypnosis is simply an altered state of consciousness. You know that feeling of being asleep on the living room couch but still being aware of where your family members are and of what's on television? And saying to yourself "I should get up and go to bed," but your body seems to weigh a ton and you can't move it?

How about the experience of waking up early and then drifting into a state that really isn't sleep? You're actually holding yourself between these two places— not getting up and going to the bathroom (which you need to do) and not drifting back to sleep. These are *hypnagogic* and *hypnopompic* states. Like hypnosis, they are altered states of consciousness. These states occur as a result of changes in brain wave patterns.

All hypnosis is essentially self-hypnosis because the individual chooses to go with the process or chooses not to. You may be saying to yourself: "I'm just not susceptible to that sort of thing. I can't be hypnotized." Well, you *choose* not to be. Actually, the more intelligent a person is, the more ability he or she has to creatively imagine, to let go and get lost in thought.

To produce a trance state, you will need an object to focus your attention on. Anything will do; something simple yet interesting, like a candle, is good. The purpose of the object is to provide an external focal point so that you can slip into a trance.

You are going to induce the trance state by convincing yourself, through self-suggestion, that you are in a trance. Select a key word or phrase that you can repeat while you are inducing the altered state of consciousness. Here are some examples:

- Down, down, down, down...
- Deeper, deeper, deeper, down, deeper...
- Heavy, heavy, heavy, very heavy...
- Further and further and further...
- I feel myself letting go, sinking and sinking, letting go...

Exercise 6

Inducing a Self-Trance

Read the steps in this exercise several times so that you can do them without referring to the book. Then actually follow the steps. The exercise will take ten to twenty minutes.

1. Select a comfortable position where you will not be disturbed.

2. Light your candle and look directly at it. Relax and open yourself up to the experience. As you look at the flame, give yourself the following instructions: "My eyelids are getting heavier and heavier. My eyelids are getting very heavy. I am ever so slowly becoming sleepy. I can't keep my eyes open."

   Accompany these instructions with full deep abdominal breathing (refer to page 38).

   There is no need to force the experience. Do not make it happen: allow it to happen gradually. Once your eyes begin to close, you are entering the beginning of the trance.

3. Now it is time to begin repeating your key phrase. These words will take you into a deeper state. Repeat your phrase over and over. Remember to stay relaxed.

4. Now begin to count backwards slowly, from 10 to 1, letting go a little more with each number. As you count, imagine going downward, deeper and deeper into the trance. You might imagine yourself going down on an elevator or sinking further and further into a cloud. You are sinking into a deep trance. Your limbs are becoming heavier and heavier.

At this point, you may want to program yourself to achieve some positive goal such as smoking cessation, weight loss, beginning an exercise program, attaining a more positive attitude, job success, or living more calmly.

5. To end the self-trance, simply give yourself the instruction: "Now, I will end my trance as I count from 1 to 10. I will wake up more with each number. When I get to 10, I will be fully awake. I will feel refreshed and energized."

Remember that the success of self-hypnosis is your attitude. Skepticism, negative expectations, fear, and anxiety will interfere. Like most things in life, if you think that hypnosis will be positive, effective, and helpful, then you will be able to enter an altered state of consciousness easily, stay in that state to accomplish your goals, and end that state without discomfort. Self-hypnosis will work for you.

When I quiet my mind, I relax my body.

Progressive Relaxation

Progressive Relaxation, as it is taught today, is actually an abbreviated form of Jacobsonian Relaxation taught by Edmond Jacobson in the 1930s. Progressive Relaxation focuses on tensing and releasing muscles, not on thoughts, feelings, or imagery. In its original form, this relaxation technique took months to learn because individuals had to spend so much time learning to feel the difference between tense and relaxed in specific muscles. In the original form, an individual might spend a month working on the forearms alone. The current form is used frequently by individuals for a variety of reasons, ranging from athletic conditioning to childbirth preparation. You can practice this very effective form of relaxation almost anywhere and at any time. Just follow the procedures in Exercise 7.

Exercise 7

Practicing
Progressive Relaxation

1. Begin by focusing on your breathing (refer to page 38).

2. Now, turn your attention to your toes. Wiggle your toes, and then, as you inhale, tense both your toes and the muscles of your feet. Hold the tension. As you exhale slowly, release the muscles of your toes and feet. Let all the tension, all the strain flow out of your toes, leaving them completely relaxed.

3. Next, turn your attention to the calves of your legs. Focus on whatever tension is stored there. As you inhale, tense your calves. Feel the tension in your shins and ankles; hold the tension. As you exhale, allow these muscles to relax; let go of whatever energy is stored there.

4. Become aware of your knees and thighs, both front and back. Notice whatever tension exists there. As you inhale, tense your thighs. Hold the tension. As you slowly exhale, let the tension go.

5. Now turn your attention to your abdomen, lower back, and buttocks. If you suffer from chronic lower back pain, you may become aware of this pain now. That's okay. This exercise will help to ease that pain. As you slowly inhale, tense your abdomen, lower back, and buttocks. Once again, feel the tension in these parts of your body. Hold the tension. As you slowly exhale, release it, letting your muscles go. Feel the warmth created by releasing these muscles.

Exercise 7

Continued

6. Next focus on your chest, shoulders, and neck. This is the area where the majority of people store tension. As you inhale, it is important to be very gentle with these parts of your body. Hold the tension in your chest and neck. Now, as you exhale, slowly release these muscles. Allow the tension to leave; feel the ever-increasing pleasant feeling of complete relaxation.

7. Notice your hands and arms. How are you holding them? Turn your palms up. As you inhale, make a fist with each hand. Feel the tension travel up your arms to your forearms and, finally, to your upper arms. Hold this tension. Now, as you exhale, release your fists, biceps, and triceps, the muscles of your arms. Feel the sensation of relaxed muscles.

8. Finally, focus on your face. People store all kinds of tension and emotion in the facial muscles. As you inhale, squish up all the muscles of your face. Hold the tension. As you exhale, let the muscles go. Release the tension and relax your face.

You have now relaxed all the major muscles of your body. This should be a very pleasant experience. Enjoy it! You will find that you have relaxed not only your body but that you also feel mentally calm. You should feel very good about what you have accomplished.

When I release tension in my body, I relax my mind.

Sound and Music

Sound, particularly music, can have a profound effect on your body. It can cause your heart rate and blood pressure to rise or your entire body to relax, lowering your vital signs and calming your mind. The human body and brain synchronize with sound. This is why people play music with a fast, hard beat when they do aerobics or jazzercise or clean the house.

In fact, some theorists believe that sound was a key to Hitler's ability to emotionally arouse large groups of people when he spoke. In Hitler's iambic pentameter style of speaking, the second of every five syllables is emphasized. (Iambic pentameter is what Shakespeare wrote in.) This beat is the rhythm of an accelerated heart rate. When people listen to it long enough, the heart begins to beat faster and people begin to feel "charged up."

Consider this. Researchers have taken groups of people who do not speak or understand a word of German and asked them to listen to a tape of Hitler. But first, a baseline measure was taken of everyone's heart rate, blood pressure, and respiratory rate. After thirty minutes of listening to the tape, participants had their vital signs taken again. Research indicated that there was a significant increase in heart rate, blood pressure, and respiratory rate after individuals had heard Hitler's voice. They had become excited. Their bodies had responded to the rhythm and fast beat of the sound.

Large companies use sound to increase productivity. Shopping malls sometimes play slower music to get shoppers to slow down and stay a while.

You can use this same concept to affect changes in your stress level. Music that is "formless"—that is, it has no foot-tapping beat or a very slow beat—induces a relaxation response. Seasoned teachers use music to calm children. Much of the old baroque music is of this kind. Some of the new synthesized music is also amorphous and effectively induces relaxation. Likewise, the sounds of the ocean or the rain elicit a relaxation response in people. Several audiocassette tapes that play nothing but the sound of the ocean or other water sounds, such as those of a babbling brook, are available. Machines that reproduce the sound of the ocean or a gentle rainstorm can also be purchased.

A very simple stress management technique is to purchase one of these tapes and play it in your car on your way to and from work, in your home, or before going to sleep at night. Exercise 8 offers an in-depth exercise using music to induce a deep state of relaxation.

Exercise 8

Achieving Relaxation
Through Music

1. Acquire a music tape that is relaxing.

2. Set aside some quiet time in a place where you won't be disturbed.

3. Start the music and dim the lights. Lie down in a comfortable position and practice deep abdominal breathing as described on page 38.

4. As you begin to relax, hear the music in a new way: hear it over the entire surface of your body, not just with your ears. Allow your entire body to hear and you will be able to experience the music as a touch sensation. The music will touch you everywhere, from the top of your head to the tip of your toes and out your fingertips. Imagine that your skin can feel the music. The music will bring you heightened awareness. Allow yourself to be totally involved in the sound as you let go. This experience will soothe and relax you.

When I let go physically, I calm my mind.

Exercise and Massage

To understand how exercise and massage can be an effective stress management tool, picture yourself as a working mother in the following situation:

You wake up in reasonable spirits, a little hurried and pressured because of an important meeting you have first thing, but basically feeling okay. One of your children informs you that today is her day to provide treats for the class— she'd forgotten all about it until now, and isn't it great that she remembered? (You want to scold her, but decide not to start the day off negatively.)

Okay, you can run to the store quickly to get treats. You return home with the goodies—but now you're behind schedule.

Finally, everyone's ready, so you get in your car to leave for the day. Oh no—a flat tire!!! You must have picked up a nail on the early morning cookie run. (You want to kick the tire and say a few choice words, but the kids are watching, and you need to set a good example about dealing with minor challenges.) Your husband has already left for work, so you're on your own here—but you're a '90s woman; you can change this tire, no problem.

Another great save, but now you're definitely running late. If you make every single light, you can probably get there within five minutes of the appointed time. The first three lights are green. "Sometimes I'm lucky!" you think. The next light is the longest wait to turn left in the city. It looks like you're going to make it . . . Your fingers tap the steering wheel in anticipation. One-one thousand, two-one thousand . . .

Oh no! The guy in front of you is distracted on his car phone and misses the turn. Now you're past the acceptable lateness grace period. (You want to honk your horn and scream something obscene, but you control yourself.) You finally arrive at work. The receptionist is definitely in an ugly mood and greets you with a snarl, informing you that the appointment you struggled to get to has been canceled. Words that you don't usually use rise up in your throat where they get stuck and stay.

In your office, you are greeted by a ringing phone. It's the school. Your son's teacher is on the phone. She wants you to come get the child immediately because he will not control his classroom antics. As the conversation progresses, your tongue begins to bleed from biting it.

It's 8:15 in the morning. You will have a head-ache by 10:00 a.m.

"Okay," you're saying to yourself. "I've had days start like that or worse. How is exercise—with everything else I have to do—going to help?"

Let's look at each of these situations as psychological experiences that you respond to physically. In the previous scenario, you have a goal—to get to a meeting on time. You are in a state of arousal because you are directing much mental and physical energy towards meeting that goal. Then you are thwarted by an obstacle, or threatened by something, like criticism, that creates a physical response. Messages, in the form of neuropeptides, are sent from your brain through your body to your muscles, preparing you to act in some way.

In some situations, you can and do act—you get the cookies and change the tire, for example. In the process of doing this, you dissipate the chemicals in your muscles, sending messages back to the brain that say, "Okay, it's dealt with." In the other situations, you choose not to take action—you don't honk at the other driver, slap the receptionist, or scream at the teacher. Although your mother would be proud, you still have all those chemicals being sent to your muscles in preparation for action—but you take no action to dissipate them, making you TENSE! You may get a headache.

Many people who go home sedate themselves with alcohol. But if you initiate some kind of action instead, such as moving your body in exercise, you can dissipate and use up those chemicals. Your body then sends messages back to the brain that allow you to "let go." You don't have to jog for five miles to accomplish this. Walk for twenty to thirty minutes when you get home, or walk the stairs at work during your lunch break. Try the Progressive Relaxation technique discussed on page 50. Break the cycle of tension. Teach your children a truly healthful way to deal with anger, frustration, and tension.

Massage works on your body in much the same way. People describe a sense of peace and well-being for several hours after receiving a massage. This feeling results because the muscles are worked by the massage therapist in a passive way. No exercise actually takes place, but the chemicals stored in the muscles are dissipated during the massage.

The majority of the world views massage as a healing tool for the mind and body. If you were under the care of a physician in Europe, for example, massage would very likely be prescribed to help you heal. It would be viewed much like a prescription or physical therapy. It is primarily in the United States that massage has seamy connotations. Professional massage therapists study the body extensively in order to relieve stress and promote healing in their patients.

Many massage therapists work by referral only. Your local phone book may also have a listing for massage therapists. You need to be discriminating when selecting one. Currently, there is no national licensure policy. Consequently, cities and states have very different qualifications for licensure. The best way to find a massage therapist is through a personal or professional referral. You might want to experiment with a few different therapists to find one you feel is most effective for you.

When you relieve physical stress, you relieve mental stress.

Diet and Nutrition

Once again, that which affects your body affects your mind. If you are careful about what you put into your body, you will not create unnecessary stress for it. Caffeine, for example, speeds up the transmission of electrical impulses in the brain. That's why drinking coffee in the morning can help you get going. However, if you find yourself jittery or restless during the day or when you try to sleep at night, caffeine may be the culprit. It is recommended that people do not take in foods or beverages with caffeine after noon. This allows your body to use up what has been taken in.

Look out for foods that are high in salt—they raise your blood pressure. Stay away from foods that are hard to digest or give you gas—that takes up energy. Eat smaller amounts of food more frequently to keep your blood sugar at an even level.

Avoid high-fat, high-calorie foods. When you put on weight, your whole system is taxed trying to service that fat. You have to manufacture more and longer capillaries to carry blood to and from the "extra" body. Your heart has to work harder, as do all your joints. Gaining weight is a very inefficient thing to do. It's not like you can add brain cells when you put on pounds. What you add is a burden.

Do you use foods to comfort yourself? Many people do. If you do, try instead some of the exercises in this book to comfort yourself. Schedule a massage for yourself. Take some time to meditate. Practice abdominal breathing. Getting calm and centered inside can take away some of the "lack" you may try to fill with comfort foods.

My mind and body are intricately connected.

Autogenic Training

Autogenic training is learning to relax by concentrating on words or phrases that you repeat either silently or aloud and then "hold" mentally for thirty to sixty seconds. Your body responds to what you say to it. Autogenics is a way to tell your body to relax. Again, the mind-body connection is at work. The autogenic training program in Exercise 9 focuses on six basic groups of statements. The first group of statements relaxes muscles. The second group of statements increases blood flow. The third and fourth groups slow heart rate and breathing. The fifth set of statements relaxes the abdomen, and the last set creates drowsiness. You should practice for about five minutes after lunch, after dinner, and before going to sleep. Start with the first set of statements. Then add the next set. Add another set each week until you are using all of them.

Exercise 9

Achieving Relaxation Through Autogenic Training

Get comfortable in a place where you won't be disturbed. Repeat each statement three times, and then hold it in your thoughts for thirty to sixty seconds.

Week 1   My right arm is heavy.
                My left arm is heavy.
                Both arms are heavy.
                My right leg is heavy.
                My left leg is heavy.
                Both legs are heavy.
                My right side is heavy.
                Everything is heavy.

Week 2   My right arm is warm.
                My left arm is warm.
                Both arms are warm.
                My right leg is warm.
                My left leg is warm.
                My arms and legs are heavy and warm.

Week 3   My heartbeat is calm and regular.

Week 4   My breathing is calm and regular.

Week 5   My abdomen is warm.

Week 6   My forehead is cool.

When I relax my body, I calm my mind.

The Six-Second Quieting Reflex

In the early 1980s, a psychologist named Charles
Stroebel combined several different stress management
methods into a procedure he called the "Quieting
Reflex." Dr. Stroebel found that this method could
begin to calm an individual down within six seconds.
But to perform this procedure effectively, you must
have practiced the techniques in the other exercises
presented throughout this book. After you have mas-
tered deep breathing (page 38), autogenics (page 61),
and Progressive Relaxation (page 50), you can put
them together for this Six-Second Quieting Reflex.

Exercise 10

Practicing the Six-Second Quieting Reflex

1. Smile inwardly with your mouth and eyes while
   telling yourself, "Alert mind, calm body."

2. Inhale an easy, natural breath.

3. Exhale and let your jaw, tongue, and shoulders go
   loose; feel a wave of limpness and warmth flow all
   the way down to your toes.

Respond to stress with relaxation.

Coping With Acute Periods of Stress and Worry

Most of the techniques described in this chapter require you to become quiet and to find calm from within. Learning the techniques and implementing them will lead you to a more healthful and peaceful way of life. But what can you do to manage acute periods of stress? Those flash-in-the-pan flare-ups that arise suddenly and sometimes without warning? Or what about those periods of intense worry over situations that you really can't control?

Remember that the body's physical response to stress is designed to prepare you to fight or run from a threat. When you become very angry with someone, your body's physical response to that stress prepares you to fight. Your anger may be very justified and necessary in order for you to set a clear boundary with the person who has angered you. But what if that someone is a three-year-old who has been whining all day and has spilled her milk . . . again? In this particular instance, your physical response may frighten both you and her.

Of the techniques described in this chapter, the Six-Second Quieting Reflex is most helpful for managing on-the-spot stress. But before you can rely on this technique for that purpose, you need plenty of practice in abdominal breathing and in learning Progressive Relaxation. If you have not fully developed the Quieting Reflex, separate yourself from the person you are intensely angry at if you feel that you may lose control. Take a walk. Go to another room. Don't approach the person until you have regained control.

Sometimes, we work ourselves to an almost crippling frenzy worrying about something that we can't control. You must face the fact that there will be times when nothing you can say or do will change a situation or a person. In those cases, you must simply accept the situation. Granted, that's easier said than done. But if you want to make a sincere effort to manage the stress in your life, you must learn to do so.

Here are two quick exercises for helping you separate yourself from persons or situations that you worry about but have no control over. These exercises aren't meant to replace proven long-term stress management techniques; they are provided to give you some immediate relief from worry.

1. Imagine putting a protective bubble around the situation or person and allowing it to drift off away from you.

2. Write the situation down on a piece of paper, put the paper in a small jar, add water, place the lid on, and put it in the freezer and leave it there.

A PERSONAL STRESS MANAGEMENT PLAN

"Learning to manage stress is not a short-term proposition. You must commit yourself to doing so."

Chapter 4

You have learned how your body responds to stress, identified some of your stressors, and learned techniques for bringing your stress under control. The next step in managing your stress is to commit to some stress management goals and to map out a plan for achieving them.

Before you begin charting your plan, let's examine three strategies that Lyle Miller, Ph.D., of the Biobehavioral Institute of Boston, offers for dealing with stressors:

1. Alter your behavior or change your perspective about a person or situation.

2. Avoid the person or situation that is causing your stress, if possible.

3. Accept things that you can't change. As discussed in Chapter 3, you can be responsible only for your own behavior. Don't waste your time and energy worrying about something that you have no control over. As much as we love certain people, we cannot make them be different than they are. Sometimes we must accept that situations are also beyond our control.

Now, examine the results of the biofeedback chart you completed in Exercise 5. Write down the people or situations that you discovered were the source of your stress. Also write down any stressors you identified as a result of completing the stress inventory in Exercise 1.

Then for each stressor you listed, consider whether you can reduce its impact by altering your behavior (perhaps using one of the techniques listed in this book), avoiding the stressor, or accepting that the person or situation can't be changed. Write how you will handle the stressor in the column marked "Coping Strategy." Be specific. If, for example, you choose to avoid the stressor, note how you will have to change your routine in order to do so. You may even wish to schedule time each day to practice the stress management techniques described in Chapter 3.

1. Sources of Stress _____
   Coping Strategy _____

2. Sources of Stress _____
   Coping Strategy _____

3. Sources of Stress _____
   Coping Strategy _____

4. Sources of Stress _____
   Coping Strategy _____

5. Sources of Stress _____
   Coping Strategy _____

6. Sources of Stress _____
   Coping Strategy _____

7. Sources of Stress _____
   Coping Strategy _____

8. Sources of Stress _____

   Coping Strategy _____

9. Sources of Stress _____

   Coping Strategy _____

10. Sources of Stress _____

    Coping Strategy _____

Remember that learning to manage the stress in your life is not a short-term proposition. You must commit yourself to doing so. Set aside a regular time for practicing the techniques in this book. Your efforts will be rewarded in the form of better health and well-being. Good luck!

BIBLIOGRAPHY AND SUGGESTED READING

Benson, Herbert. *The Relaxation Response.* New York: Morrow, 1975.

Bliss, Shepherd, ed. *The New Holistic Health Handbook: Living Will in a New Age.* Lexington, MA: S. Greene Press, 1985.

Blythe, Peter. *Stress Disease, The Growing Plague.* New York: St. Martin's Press, 1981.

Brown, Barbara, B. *New Mind, New Body; Biofeedback: New Directions for the Mind.* New York: Harper & Row, 1974.

Dudley, Denise M. *Every Woman's Guide to Career Success.* Mission, KS: SkillPath Publications, 1991.

Friedman, Paul. *How to Deal With Difficult People.* Mission, KS: SkillPath Publications, 1989.

Hemingway, Patricia D. *The Transcendental Meditation Primer: How to Stop Tension and Start Living.* New York: D. McKay, 1975.

Miller, Lyle H., and Alma Dell Smith with Larry Rothstein. "Your Personal Stress Action Plan." *Executive Female* (May/June 1993): 29-35.

Olton, David S., and Aaron R. Noonberg. *Biofeedback: Clinical Applications in Behavioral Medicine.* Englewood Cliffs, NJ: Prentice-Hall, 1980.

Pelletier, Kenneth R. *Mind As Healer, Mind As Slayer: A Holistic Approach to Preventing Stress Disorders.* New York: Dell, 1977.

Poley, Michelle Fairfield. *A Winning Attitude: How to Develop Your Most Important Asset!* Mission, KS: SkillPath Publications, 1992.

Selye, Hans, M.D. *The Stress of Life.* New York: McGraw-Hill, 1956.

Selye, Hans, M.D. *Stress Without Distress.* Philadelphia: Lippincott, 1974.

Shealy, Norman C. *90 Days to Self-Health.* New York: Dial Press, 1977.

Shealy, C. Norman, and Caroline M. Myss. *Aids: Passageway to Transformation.* Walpole, NH: Stillpoint Publications, 1988.

Sheridan, Charles L., and Sally A. Ramacer. *Health Psychology: Challenging the Biomedical Model.* New York: John Wiley & Sons, 1992.

Siegel, Bernie S., M.D., *Peace, Love and Healing Bodymind Communication and the Path to Self-Healing: An Exploration.* New York: Harper & Row, 1989.

Solomon, G.F. "A Psychoneuroimmunology: Interactions Between Central Nervous System and Immune System." *Journal of Neuroscience Research* 18 (1987):1-9.

Temme, Jim. *Productivity Power: 250 Great Ideas for Being More Productive.* Mission, KS: SkillPath Publications, 1993.